HEINEMANN GUIDED READERS
UPPER LEVEL

Series Editor: John Milne

Readers at *Upper Level* are intended as an aid to students which will start them on the road to reading unsimplified books in the whole range of English literature. At the same time, the content and language of the Readers at Upper Level are carefully controlled with the following main features:

Information Control   As at other levels in the series, information which is vital to the development of a story is carefully presented in the text and then reinforced through the *Points for Understanding* section. Some background references may be unfamiliar to students, but these are explained in the text and in notes in the *Glossary*. Care is taken with pronoun reference.

Structure Control   Students can expect to meet those structures covered in any basic English Course. Particularly difficult structures, such as complex nominal groups and embedded clauses, are used sparingly. Clauses and phrases within sentences are carefully balanced and sentence length is limited to a maximum of four clauses in nearly all cases.

Vocabulary Control   At Upper Level, there is a basic vocabulary of approximately 2,200 words. At the same time students are given the opportunity to meet new words, including some simple idiomatic and figurative English usages which are clearly explained in the *Glossary*.

Gym

D1677559

Guided Readers at Upper Level

JOHN BYRNE

The Story of Pop

HEINEMANN EDUCATIONAL BOOKS
LONDON

Heinemann Educational Books Ltd

LONDON   EDINBURGH   MELBOURNE   AUCKLAND   TORONTO
HONG KONG   SINGAPORE   KUALA LUMPUR
IBADAN   NAIROBI   JOHANNESBURG
LUSAKA   NEW DELHI   KINGSTON

ISBN 0 435 27025 7

Cover by London Features International Limited

Published by
Heinemann Educational Books Ltd,
48 Charles Street, London W1X 8AH

Filmset in Photon Times 12 pt by
Richard Clay (The Chaucer Press), Ltd, Bungay, Suffolk
and printed in Great Britain by
Fletcher & Son Ltd, Norwich

Contents

Glossary

The glossary at the back of this book on page 83 is divided into four sections. A number beside a word in the text, like this [3], refers to a section of the glossary. *Section 1* – a list of the types of pop music – is only referred to once in the text. Within each section, the words and phrases are listed in alphabetical order.

Section 1 – list of types of pop music
Section 2 – terms to do with music and the music industry
Section 3 – adjectives used to describe music and musicians
Section 4 – other words

ONE

ROCK AROUND THE CLOCK

It was very early one dark spring morning in 1973. A number of young girls, most of them about the age of twelve or thirteen, were waiting in the main hall of London airport. They passed the time drinking coffee and eating sandwiches. Some of them were talking and some were reading. Now and then, one or two of them got up and walked around impatiently before sitting down again.

All the time, more and more girls were arriving at the airport and soon there was a really large crowd. One girl who had just arrived recognised a friend in the middle of the crowd.

'Hi, Jane,' she shouted.

'Hi, Susan,' came the reply. 'Been here long?'

'Since six o'clock. We've been here more than two hours. They should arrive soon. It can't be long now because . . .'

Her words were lost in the tremendous noise of a plane coming in to land at London airport. Immediately everybody rushed to the big windows. There were photographers and newspaper reporters everywhere, taking photographs and writing down notes. Many of the girls rushed outside to try to get nearer the plane. Its doors opened and six young boys stepped out.

Well, of course, they were the Osmonds. In 1973, no other group in the world of entertainment could have brought such a crowd of fans [2] to the airport. Next day, the newspapers said there had never been a welcome like it before. Perhaps the journalists did not remember as much as the men who had worked at the airport for many years.

These men were able to remember many similar scenes, with the same large crowds of fans and the same ex-

The younger faces of pop in the seventies – the Osmonds.

citement. For example, the best known group of all, the Beatles, had received this kind of welcome many times in the past.

In 1957, the first American rock 'n' roll[1] singer who came to England, Bill Haley, had arrived by boat in Southampton. A very large crowd of fans was waiting to meet him. Later he travelled to London in a special train almost as if he had been a king or a president!

Naturally, everyone read about these events in the newspapers and watched them on TV. At the same time a film which included pop[2] music was being widely talked about in newspapers and on TV. The film was called *The Blackboard Jungle*. In this film Bill Haley and the Comets played and sang a song called *Rock around the Clock*. In many ways this song marked the beginning of 'pop'.

How has pop developed since then? To answer this question, we must look at some of the changes which have

America's first rock 'n' roll star – Bill Haley with the Comets.

taken place in society and music since the 1950s. In America, round about the year 1955, a type of music known as 'rock 'n' roll' first became popular, especially among young people.

In the early fifties, not many young people bought records. They did not have much money and the only popular music was the music which their parents liked. Perhaps you have heard that kind of music. For example, a large band, often with a singer, played well-known romantic [3] music to which couples danced simple, popular dances like the waltz.

Everything was done very politely and quietly and young people had to listen to the same music as their parents. Some liked it and others did not. But, even if they did not like it, there was nothing else to listen to. There were no records which young people really wanted to buy.

Immediately after the Second World War, Europe and

America faced great economic difficulties, but by about 1955 America had solved its problems. In the fifties, America had become richer than ever before. At the same time, the political situation in the world was extremely confused.

America and Russia were enemies and seemed to be ready to use the terrible power of the atomic bomb. Many young people were troubled by this situation. On the one hand, their society promised a great future; on the other hand, there was the danger of total destruction. So, in many ways, they could not accept the world of their parents.

At the same time, the music and interests of the older generation was boring to young people who realised that their world might be destroyed at any moment. In America, the richest country in the world, there were lots of young people with money to spend. And they could only spend their money on the same things as their parents.

So, although teenagers had money, they could not spend it as they wanted. They were expected to wear the same kind of clothes that their parents had worn when they were teenagers.

Whenever young people have enough money, they become independent. And naturally, they want to show that they are independent and can make their own decisions. They can show this independence by the sort of clothes they wear. They can also find their own music to replace the old-fashioned[3] music of their parents.

The men who controlled the record companies realised that teenagers were looking for a different kind of music. But they did not really know what young people wanted. And so these men began to make records of many new singers, hoping to find the type of music which appealed to teenagers.

They found the right music almost by accident in the

4

film *Blackboard Jungle*. As the film began, the audience heard Bill Haley and the Comets play *Rock around the Clock*. Teenagers who went to see the film heard the song and they bought millions of copies of the record.

Rock around the Clock was the first song which really belonged to teenagers. It was the beginning of rock 'n' roll. Since then pop has grown into a very rich industry. Young people spend huge amounts of money on records, cassettes, concerts and magazines. They spend money on anything connected with their favourite music and musicians. In this way, young people have helped to create pop and make it the special music of young people all over the world.

ROCK 'N' ROLL

Before Bill Haley arrived in England, he was already famous. *Rock around the Clock* had already sold more than a million copies [2] and *Blackboard Jungle* had received a lot of comment and criticism. So when he arrived in England in 1957, he immediately became the centre of attention in the newspapers and on TV.

He toured [2] England with his group, the Comets, and gave concerts in most big cities. Everywhere great crowds came to listen to him. Most people enjoyed his music so much that they got up and danced in the spaces between the seats. A year earlier, young people had danced in the cinemas in the same way to the music of the film, *Blackboard Jungle.*

It was clear that something important was happening. Nobody could remember anything like it. Of course, there had always been popular songs and singers, and these singers had had great numbers of fans. But the young people at Bill Haley's concerts behaved in a way which showed more than just enjoyment. It showed that they wanted to rebel against their parents and against older people in general.

Bill Haley and other rock 'n' roll singers annoyed many older people in several ways. For example, older people thought rock 'n' roll was noisy and unpleasant. And it really was very different from the quieter, romantic love songs which had been popular before.

The style of dancing to rock 'n' roll was called 'jiving', and older people found it strange. When a couple 'jived', they did not dance close together; they jumped up and down, and turned around and threw each other in the air. Most parents disliked the new kind of music

Jiving – nothing like the older types of dancing.

because of the noise and the way the young people danced.

There was one more problem – the clothes worn by the rock 'n' roll singers who came from America. Young people had always worn the same kind of clothes as their parents. They had cut their hair in the same way as their parents, too. When rock 'n' roll appeared, the problems of hair and clothes came with it. The American singers wore their hair much longer than ordinary people, and they preferred jeans and tee-shirts. They did not like wearing ties, either. In England, in 1955, almost every man and boy had to wear a tie and almost everybody had short hair.

And then one day a teenager went to school with longer hair, trying to look like his favourite singer. His headmaster immediately sent him home from school and told him to get his hair cut. The incident made a good story for the newspapers, and the same thing happened several times in the following months.

Journalists saw these events as the beginning of a conflict between the generations. The older generation preferred ordinary clothes and the music they had always been used to. The younger generation was starting to prefer different, more colourful clothes, and a new, more exciting kind of music.

The newspapers found a special phrase to describe what was happening. This phrase was 'the generation gap'. It expressed the big difference between the tastes and opinions of the older generation and the tastes and opinions of young people.

Money helped to make the 'generation gap' wider. As America and Western Europe became richer and richer, there was more money and more work for everybody, especially young people. And so, with all this money, a teenager could show his independence in many ways: for example in his clothes and in his favourite music.

Teddy boys at a rock 'n' roll concert at Wembley Stadium, London.

In rock 'n' roll, and in the new clothes and actions, people could hear and see the generation gap. Most people were interested in the events which were taking place. Some people felt that their authority was in danger and they did not like these changes at all.

But there was another group of people who welcomed the changes. These were the people who worked on newspapers and TV and those who made films or records. Journalists found many good stories in the new events. For example, newspapers frequently had stories about groups of teenage boys known as 'Teddy Boys'.

'Teddy Boys' dressed in clothes like those worn in England during the time of King Edward VII at the beginning of this century. The King had been known as 'Teddy' and this name was used to describe these young men. People noticed the strange clothes of the Teddy Boys and stared at them in the street.

Teddy Boys liked rock 'n' roll and they went to concerts and cinemas in large numbers to hear their favourite music. They often caused trouble and sometimes they started to fight. Many people were afraid of the Teddy Boys. And, of course, these people did not like their music, either.

As well as comment in newspapers, several films were made about the generation gap. *Blackboard Jungle* was one of these films. It is a story about the problems of teachers and students in the violent schools in New York City. In the cinema, the new stars were James Dean and Marlon Brando. Both appeared in films about the problems of young people.

The titles of these films are interesting. James Dean's film was called *Rebel without a Cause* and Dean himself played the rebel. Brando appeared in a film called *The Wild Ones*, which was about a group of violent young men who rode around on big, powerful motorbikes. Neither Brando or Dean looked like a Hollywood star of the forties and both had large numbers of young fans.

In the music business[2], record producers for the big companies were also looking for new stars. They wanted to find more songs like *Rock around the Clock* and also singers who could sing this new kind of music.

But what do we know about this new music? Rock 'n' roll was a mixture of different types of earlier music which had taken a long time to develop. In the next chapter we will look at where it came from and how it grew.

THREE

RHYTHM 'N' BLUES

In the seventeenth and eighteenth centuries, thousands of black people were brought from West Africa to work as slaves in the cotton fields of America. These slaves had their own kind of music and they sang together as they worked in the fields. They sang about their sadness and their songs had regular rhythms[2] which helped them to work together. African musical ideas, great feeling and strong rhythm together created a kind of singing which was called 'the blues'. The blues are the real folk[2] songs of the American negro.

After the Civil War in America (1861–1865), slavery was abolished and negroes were free. Now a negro was allowed to learn to play some of the white man's musical instruments, like the piano, the trumpet or the clarinet. Soon black musicians were playing the blues on these instruments. This new kind of music was called jazz.

When white people heard jazz, they disliked it very much. They were shocked because jazz was noisy and rhythmic[3] and very different from their own favourite music. White people preferred quiet, romantic music. They attacked jazz in the same way that they attacked rock 'n' roll fifty years later.

Although white people never accepted jazz in its original[3] noisy form, it became very popular during the twenties and thirties. White orchestras used the melodies[2] and rhythms of jazz, but added violins to make the music sweeter. White singers sang the new music in their old-fashioned way and jazz gradually became more acceptable to the tastes of white people.

Among themselves, American negroes still played real jazz. And they still sang the blues. Their lives had

12

improved a little, but the negroes were still the poorest people of America. They still needed the blues to express their pain and sadness.

During the nineteenth century, negroes lived and worked in the southern states of America. But in the 1920s, there was a great economic depression and it became almost impossible to find a job in the south. The men had to travel to northern cities like Chicago and New York in order to find work. And they often had to leave their wives and children behind them.

These negroes were living and working under strange, new conditions. They were lonely and sad. Naturally, they used to meet together in the evening to talk and also to sing and play their own music — the blues and jazz. They sang about their loneliness and their sadness. But the negroes sang among themselves and very few white people ever heard their music.

But this situation changed completely after the end of the Second World War. There were two important reasons for this change: the invention of the electric guitar and the development of a large number of radio stations all over America.

The electric guitar was much more powerful than the ordinary guitar and much louder. Also, together with a pianist and a drummer, a good musician could play music which made people want to dance. The new sound had a strong, exciting rhythm and so this type of music was called 'rhythm 'n' blues'.

In America, there were different radio stations for black and white listeners. There were also records of jazz and blues by black musicians, which were made especially for the negroes. White people, of course, did not listen to black radio stations or buy these records.

Perhaps by chance, a few young white boys and girls heard rhythm 'n' blues on their radios. Most of them did not like it at first, but a small number found it more

13

exciting than any other music they had heard before. Naturally, they told their friends about rhythm 'n' blues. In the years after the war, there was a growing audience of young white teenagers who listened to black music and enjoyed it.

When their parents found out about their interest in rhythm 'n' blues, they were not pleased. They could not understand why teenagers preferred the music of the negroes. Negroes were the poorest people in America and were much disliked by many white people. And, of course, many parents expected their children to have the same tastes and ideas as themselves.

We have already seen, however, that young people will try to be independent if they are given the opportunity. They want to choose their own clothes, their own music and their own way of life. The tastes of young people are often different from those of their parents, especially if the young people have money of their own.

In America at this time, there was another kind of popular music called 'country 'n' western'. In the same way that the blues was the music of the black people, country 'n' western was the music of the poorer white farmers. For these farmers, country music expressed their feelings about life, just as the blues had done for the negro.

Country music did not have the strong rhythm and excitement of rhythm 'n' blues, but it was full of simple, enjoyable melodies. Country music, too, had its own records and its own radio programmes. Like the blues, it was most popular in the farming areas in the southern states of America.

In these states, like Alabama and Georgia, black and white people lived in the same towns and worked on the same farms. Young people who grew up in these places naturally heard both country music and the blues. Many white teenagers liked rhythm 'n' blues because it made them want to dance, but they preferred the words and melodies of country music. They did not really like or understand the sadness of the blues.

When they played music for their own enjoyment, they added the rhythms of black music to country music. The result was the type of music we call rock 'n' roll. Bill Haley was the first to make it popular with *Rock around the Clock*. Soon other rock 'n' roll singers tried to follow his success.

In my own opinion, black musicians have always played the most exciting rock 'n' roll. Black musicians such as Chuck Berry, Little Richard and Bo Diddley were the real masters of rock 'n' roll, but most white people in America would not buy records made by black singers.

White rock 'n' roll was usually more influenced[2] by country music than the blues. And white singers never seemed to produce the same strong feeling of rhythm and excitement as black musicians. White singers like Elvis Presley, Buddy Holly and Eddie Cochran made some very memorable records, but the best of them all was Jerry Lee Lewis.

Rock 'n' roll was only popular in England for a short time. English teenagers did not have as much money to spend as young people in America. Their parents still bought more records and these older people wanted to listen to familiar[3], old-fashioned music.

By 1962, everybody seemed to have forgotten rock 'n' roll. English popular music continued in its old-fashioned way. Large bands played soft dance music on the radio and the hit parade[2] was full of quiet, romantic songs. The noise and excitement of rock 'n' roll gradually disappeared and nothing had really changed at all. But we had not heard the Beatles – yet!

Elvis Presley – a universal star in the history of pop.

Chuck Berry – one of the real masters of rock 'n' roll.

FOUR

THE BEATLES

One cold Saturday morning in November 1963, I was sitting by the fire reading a newspaper, when there was a knock at the door. I went to open it and my friend, Judy, rushed into the room. She seemed very excited.

'What's the matter?' I asked.

'Nothing's the matter,' she replied. 'Just the opposite. I've got two tickets for the Beatles' concert on Monday night.'

'You've got two tickets for the Beatles!' I exclaimed, 'How did you manage that? Did you rob a bank or something?'

Judy laughed and told me how she had managed to get the tickets. It was very simple. Judy worked as a reporter on the local newspaper. She had been able to get tickets because she was going to write about the concert for the newspaper.

As you can imagine, I was delighted. Two days earlier, I had cycled past the theatre where the Beatles were going to appear. There had been a long queue of Beatle fans, waiting to buy tickets for the concert. The queue began outside the theatre, ran along the street and disappeared round the corner. Although I wanted to see the Beatles very much, I did not have enough time to wait for a ticket and so I had tried to forget about the concert.

A year earlier, in 1962, the Beatles had made their first record. It was called *Love Me Do*. Only a year later, they were the most famous pop group in the world.

Love Me Do did not reach the top of the 'charts'[2], but both their second and third records did. These songs, *Love Me Do*, *From Me to You* and *Please, Please Me* were all written by John Lennon and Paul McCartney. In

Four boys from Liverpool. The Beatles in the Cavern days.

addition to Lennon and McCartney, the other members of the Beatles were George Harrison and later Ringo Starr.

Because Lennon and McCartney wrote so many good songs, the Beatles always had enough material to sing and record. In this way they avoided one of the biggest problems of many groups: the problem of finding a good song for their next record. On their L.P.s [2] the Beatles occasionally recorded songs written by other people, but usually other singers and groups wanted to record Lennon and McCartney songs.

All the members of the Beatles were born in Liverpool, a big city in the north of England. Ringo was the oldest, born in July 1940, and George the youngest, born in February 1943. They all went to school in Liverpool and, as boys, they listened to and liked the same kind of music.

They met each other in clubs and shared a common interest in rock 'n' roll. Instead of just listening, they soon decided to play their favourite kind of music themselves. At first they practised together and played in local clubs whenever they could.

It was difficult to get jobs playing their kind of music in clubs in Liverpool, so the Beatles accepted work in Hamburg, in Germany. They went there in 1960 and stayed for more than a year. In Hamburg they worked very hard, playing in clubs every night of the week. When they returned to Liverpool in 1962, they were already very skilful musicians. In those two years, they had learnt how to write good songs and play them well.

Back in Liverpool, they played at a club called 'The Cavern'. Soon, young people in that city began talking about the Beatles. More and more of these teenagers went to listen to the Beatles when they played at The Cavern. In Liverpool itself, they were already famous.

Then one day, a girl went into a big music shop in Liverpool. She asked the manger if he had a record by a group called 'the Beatles'. The manager told her that the

Beatles had never made a record. During the next few weeks many more people came into the shop to ask for a Beatles' record. Each time the manager had to tell them the same thing: the Beatles had not made a record.

The manager of the music shop was called Brian Epstein. Because so many people had asked for a record by the Beatles, Epstein decided to go and listen to the group himself. When he heard them, he was astonished at first by the noise in the small club. But soon, like everybody else in The Cavern, he began to enjoy himself.

Brian Epstein enjoyed himself so much that he spoke to the Beatles when they had finished playing. He talked to them for a long time and finally persuaded them to let him become their manager. He knew a lot about the music industry [2] and so would be able to help them in their career.

Epstein wrote to all the big record companies and sent them tapes of the Beatles singing and playing. The record companies did not really like the Beatles' music. At first, nobody wanted to give them the chance to make a record.

But, in his office in London, one important man listened again and again to the tapes. He felt sure that the Beatles would be successful. This man's name was George Martin, and he persuaded his record company to give the Beatles a chance to make a record. That was just the beginning.

George Martin knew a lot about music and the best way to record it. So, when the Beatles began to make records, they needed Martin's advice and help. Together they recorded *Love Me Do* and *Please, Please Me* and all their other early hits.

At the same time, the Beatles started to tour England, giving concerts all over the country. On their first tour, they appeared with many other groups, many of them better known than the Beatles. Only two months later, in May 1963, they made another tour of Britain. This time they were the most famous names in the show. By the end of the year everybody was talking about the Beatles, reading about them in the newspapers and buying their records.

Then, Judy and I read that the Beatles were coming to our town to give a concert. And a few days later, we were standing outside the theatre, holding our precious tickets for the Beatles' concert. It was like a dream. We almost could not believe it!

Inside the theatre, people moved around impatiently and talked excitedly. Suddenly the lights went down and we looked into the darkness. We saw a movement behind the curtains. They opened and a man stepped out to introduce the first group. I have forgotten who they were because we were all waiting for the second part of the show. We wanted to see the Beatles.

We were too afraid to leave our seats during the interval because we did not want to lose them. It seemed a long time before the lights went down again and the theatre became dark. As the curtains were drawn back, we could not hear either the announcer or even the music. But there, on stage, were the Beatles.

The noise was astonishing. Everywhere in the theatre, girls were screaming and crying, or jumping up and down and waving at the four young men on the stage. For more than half an hour it was impossible to hear what the Beatles were playing. Suddenly they stopped playing and John Lennon announced that they were going to sing their new record, *I Want to Hold Your Hand*.

Oh yeh   I'll tell you something
I think you'll understand
Then I'll say that something
I wanna hold your hand
I wanna hold your hand
I wanna hold your hand

(from *I Want to Hold Your Hand*)

Strangely, the theatre became silent because we all wanted to hear their new song. Well, perhaps you know that more people bought a copy of *I Want to Hold Your Hand* than any other Beatles' record. When we heard it that night for the first time, it was unforgettable.

Shortly after the concert I went to see Judy, I had bought her the record of *I Want to Hold Your Hand*. It was a way of thanking her for taking me with her to the concert. I gave her the record and said:

'I hope you like it. It'll help you to remember the concert.'

'That's funny,' she replied.

Judy went to the table and picked up a record which was lying there. She gave it to me and said,

'I had exactly the same idea!'

It was, of course, a copy of *I Want to Hold Your Hand*.

FIVE

BRITISH GROUPS IN THE SIXTIES

Before the success of the Beatles, pop music had been dominated by America. Rock 'n' roll came from America. It was American teenagers with their money and interest who had helped pop music to grow. In England, musical ideas followed those of America, but only some time later. Teenagers in England still did not have very much money. They also had very little contact with American rock 'n' roll and country music.

There are two cities in England which had more contact with America than any others. One city, of course, was London, which had visitors not only from America, but from all over the world. The other city was Liverpool. Liverpool has a very large port and ships sailed regularly between Liverpool and America.

Some young people in Liverpool were able to get records of American music from the sailors and travellers on these ships. It was almost impossible to find records like these in music shops in England.

In Liverpool, there were already many groups playing rhythm 'n' blues. They had listened very carefully to the original American records and had learnt to play in the same way. After he had discovered the Beatles, Brian Epstein found out that there were other pop groups in Liverpool playing the same kind of music.

Some of them were immediately successful under his management. These groups often had their first hits because they recorded Lennon and McCartney songs. But they could not use the two Beatles as their song-writers for ever. Without good, new songs, the popularity of these groups lasted only a short time.

In the early sixties, many groups suddenly appeared,

and disappeared just as quickly. But a few really outstanding [3] groups did become known. Two of them, the Rolling Stones and the Who, have carried on into the seventies. Another group, the Animals, broke up in 1966, but for three years they were almost as popular as the Beatles and Rolling Stones.

The Animals came from Newcastle, another seaport in the north of England. People called them 'animals' because they were so wild and noisy on stage. Their singer, Eric Burdon, admired and understood black music and the group as a whole played strong, exciting rhythm 'n' blues.

Apart from the Beatles, the Rolling Stones were probably the best known and most successful group in pop music. They had their first hit a few months after the Beatles and their second record was a Lennon and McCartney song, *I Wanna be your Man*. Although many people thought that the Rolling Stones were similar to the Beatles, they were different in some important ways.

At first, the Beatles' long hair had caused a lot of surprise and comment, but soon most people, even the older generation, accepted them. In spite of their long hair, the Beatles were pleasant and attractive, spoke intelligently in public and were polite to everybody. They seemed to be ordinary young men with extraordinary musical talent [2].

The Rolling Stones, by comparison, made a lot of people angry. Their hair was even longer than the Beatles', their clothes were strange and they did not try to be polite to journalists and interviewers. The older generation, especially, did not like their music, which was very much in the style of the blues.

I went to see the Rolling Stones in 1963, at the beginning of their career. In the middle of the River Thames near London, there is a small island, called Eel Pie Island. On this island there was an enormous, dark old house. In

Mick Jagger and the Rolling Stones – loud, noisy and loved by their fans.

the early sixties, the Rolling Stones often played there on Sunday nights.

There were no other houses on the island and no lights along the road. It seemed a very lonely place. We crossed an old bridge in the darkness and made our way carefully towards the black shape of the old house. As we got nearer, the noise became louder and louder. Suddenly we were in the middle of the noise itself, among the very large crowd in the old house.

The only light in the whole building shone on the stage where we could see the Rolling Stones. Their appearance was really extraordinary. We had never seen such long hair, nor such strange, old clothes. For more than a year before their first hit, the Rolling Stones had earned very little money. They had borrowed old clothes and bought second-hand coats which did not fit them and so they looked very strange.

Their music was even stranger. I had never heard the kind of music they were playing. It sounded completely different from the pop music we usually heard on the radio. The Rolling Stones were playing real rhythm 'n' blues. They had listened to the records of black musicians like Muddy Waters, Bo Diddley and Chuck Berry, and had learnt to play their songs in the same way.

At first we did not enjoy their music because it was so loud and so unusual. But after listening to the Rolling Stones several times, we started to understand and like it. Many other people, too, began to enjoy their kind of rhythm 'n' blues and the Rolling Stones had their first hit record late in 1963. It was a Chuck Berry song called *Come On*.

From that time their popularity grew and grew, until they were almost as popular as the Beatles. In spite of their new popularity, the Rolling Stones had problems in other ways. For example, they were in trouble with the police on several occasions. In 1966 Mick Jagger and

Keith Richard were arrested at a party and accused of having drugs.

It was a good story for the newspapers. Journalists used the opportunity to describe the Rolling Stones as rebels against society. The judge at their trial sent Mick Jagger and Keith Richard to prison for a year, but a higher court changed their punishment to a large fine instead. Those people who had disliked the Rolling Stones at first now began to criticise them even more.

As well as Mick Jagger and Keith Richard, another member of the group, Brian Jones, also got into trouble with the police. He, too, was arrested twice and accused of having drugs. On each occasion he was found guilty and fined a lot of money.

In spite of all these problems, the Rolling Stones continued to make exciting records. Many of these records, like *Honky Tonk Woman*, *Jumping Jack Flash* and *Satisfaction* were not only great hits for the group, but were also recorded by many other singers. These songs were written by Mick Jagger and Keith Richard. Although the Rolling Stones had used other writers' songs at first, they soon discovered that their own songs were just as good.

In July 1969, Brian Jones left the group. A few weeks later, he drowned in the swimming pool of his new home after a midnight swim. He died only two days before the Rolling Stones gave their famous free concert in Hyde Park, London. Twenty-five thousand people listened silently as Mick Jagger read a poem in memory of Brian Jones.

The following year, the Rolling Stones played at another festival at Altamont, California. Large, open-air concerts had become popular because of the success of pop festivals like those on the Isle of Wight and at Woodstock.

On these occasions there were usually so many pop

fans that it was difficult to control them. Often there was conflict between the fans and the police. Sometimes there were also groups of tough young men who rode large, powerful motorbikes. They were called 'Hell's Angels'.

Hell's Angels at the 1969 open-air concert in Hyde Park.

The Hell's Angels enjoyed fighting and liked to annoy the peaceful pop fans at the festivals. The Rolling Stones tried to avoid this problem by asking the Hell's Angels themselves to control the crowds. Everybody hoped that this would keep the Hell's Angels busy and would prevent them from making trouble.

29

But at Altamont the plan went wrong. Some young fans tried to get too close to the stage where the Rolling Stones were playing. The Hell's Angels forced the fans back and fighting broke out. While Mick Jagger was singing and the group was playing, one young man was killed in the fighting. Another fan was seriously hurt. At the same time, a few metres away on the stage, the music carried on.

In the seventies, the Rolling Stones have played at more concerts and have made more good records. Another group, the Who, has continued into the seventies, even though they began to play together as long ago as 1964. The Who had their first hit in 1965 with a song called *Can't Explain*, and since then they have got better and better.

They were first noticed because they wore unusual clothes and were often photographed in Carnaby Street[4], dressed in the latest fashions. Later they became known as the group who smashed their instruments to pieces at the end of each show.

In spite of all this publicity, the Who would not have been successful if they had not had real musical talent. They give really exciting concerts, but the songs of Pete Townshend have also helped to make them one of the most popular groups in the world. Pete Townshend is the group's guitarist and he wrote the music for the Who's most famous works[2], *Tommy* and *Quadrophenia*.

Tommy was the first 'Rock Opera'. It was called an 'opera' because it tells the story, in music and songs, of a deaf, blind and dumb boy called Tommy. In 1975, *Tommy* was made into a very successful film. *Quadrophenia* also tells a story about the life of a young rebel in England in the early sixties. As well as their two 'operas', the Who have also given us some great hit songs like *My Generation* and *I Can See for Miles*.

Most of the other British groups who were so popular

during the sixties have either broken up or stopped playing. But in the twentieth century we are lucky, because with records and the radio, we can listen again and again to some of the best music of the sixties.

SIX

BOB DYLAN

In the summer of 1963, I received a letter from a friend in America. In this letter, he asked me if I had heard of a singer called Bob Dylan. My friend said that he had been listening to a record of a singer who could not sing very well and who played the guitar and mouth organ rather badly. But the singer, Bob Dylan, had interested him more than any other singer he had ever heard.

At that time in England, only the Beatles seemed important. I had never heard of Bob Dylan. However, during the next two years I began to hear his name more and more as his songs were recorded and made popular by other singers and groups. Probably the best known of all his songs was *Blowing in the Wind* which became an enormous hit all over the world in 1964.

Bob Dylan's real name was Robert Zimmerman and he was born in Duluth, Minnesota (U.S.A.) in 1941. When he began to sing and write songs, he changed his name to Dylan because of his admiration for Dylan Thomas. Dylan Thomas was a Welsh poet who was very popular in America at that time. Although Bob Dylan got a place at University to study literature, he left after six months and went to New York. He wanted to become a singer.

In New York, Dylan met Woody Guthrie. Guthrie was a folk-singer of an earlier generation, who by this time was seriously ill in hospital. Although he was very ill, Guthrie helped and encouraged the young singer. In his first album[2], in 1961, Dylan included a *Song to Woody* to show his respect and thanks for the older singer's help.

Even though Dylan's first album did not sell a great number of copies, it was enough to make people pay attention to him. He had an unusual voice. It sounded as if

Bob Dylan. The American folk hero.

he was singing through his nose and he had an unusual way of playing the mouth organ. Before Dylan, people played the mouth organ by blowing only, but Dylan changed this. He played it both blowing and sucking.

On Dylan's second album, *The Freewheelin' Bob Dylan*, there was a song that really made him successful. The song was *Blowing in the Wind*. Personally, I do not think that it is one of his best songs. But its world-wide popularity made Bob Dylan's name so well known that people began to listen to everything he sang or wrote.

After *Blowing in the Wind*, Dylan wrote some other really good songs like *It Ain't Me, Babe* and *Don't Think Twice, It's Alright*, as well as a number of political songs. Perhaps you have heard the anti-war songs, *Masters of War* and *With God on our Side*. And you may have heard the song about the rebellion of the young against the world of their parents. This song was called *The Times They Are A-Changin'*.

'Come mothers and fathers,
Throughout the land
And don't criticize
What you can't understand.
Your sons and your daughters
Are beyond your command
Your old road is
Rapidly agin'
Please get out of the new one
If you can't lend your hand
For the times they are a-changin' '

(from *The Times They Are A-Changin'*)

The song says that the world is changing so quickly that the older generation cannot understand what is happening. Dylan tells parents that 'your sons and daughters are beyond your command' and that the older generation should not try to stop progress and change.

Such ideas were simple and direct and appealed strongly to young people everywhere. And this was especially true in America. Many people there were beginning to disagree with the American part in the Vietnam war. In his song, *The Times They Are A-Changin'*, Dylan expressed the feelings of young people who wanted to make the world a better place to live in.

These songs contained political and social ideas, but they were not difficult either to sing or play. The tunes were easy to remember and the words and ideas, although powerful, were simply expressed. Anyone who was able to play the guitar a little could learn the songs very quickly. Dylan's songs were easy to sing and this was one of the reasons for his popularity.

By 1965, Dylan was so successful that a lot of people began to imitate him. And so 'folk' became a movement within pop music. Although the Beatles still sold more records than anyone else, perhaps Dylan changed pop even more than they did.

Dylan made words important. Although rock 'n' roll had brought many changes to popular music, it had not changed the kind of words used in the songs. These words were as simple and unimaginative as they had always been. Even the Beatles were still writing songs about the same old situations.

Dylan, almost alone, changed all this and made people listen to the words of a song. Words were important to Dylan. As a schoolboy, he had read a lot of poetry and this influenced many of his songs.

Dylan also wrote songs attacking war and exploitation [4]. Many of his songs were about these kinds of problems in America. For example, *Oxford Town* was about the problem of violence between negroes and white people. *A Hard Rain's Gonna Fall* was an angry song about the dangerous quarrel between America and Russia about Cuba in 1962.

In his love songs, most of all, you felt that he was trying to speak sincerely. He refused to write the old-fashioned kind of teenage love songs. Instead, he tried to express all sorts of different and complex[3] feelings.

For example, in *It Ain't Me, Babe*, he says to the girl: 'I am not really the person you are looking for because I can't give you what you want. I like you very much, but I can't say any more than that.' This kind of honesty appealed to young people. Other writers and singers realised this and began to follow Dylan's example.

Dylan succeeded in changing pop music for the better. He opened the door for intelligent song-writers like Joan Baez, Tom Paxton and Paul Simon, and later Leonard Cohen and Joni Mitchell. Even the Beatles were influenced by Dylan and we can see this influence in songs like *Eleanor Rigby* and *She's Leaving Home*.

Meanwhile, Dylan's own music had changed. He started playing and singing with a rock 'n' roll group called The Band. Now, one of the beliefs of the folk movement is that music and song belong to everybody. Folk music must be able to be played and enjoyed by everybody who wishes to share in it. For example, folk singers did not use electric equipment which was very expensive.

Many fans of folk music thought that Dylan had betrayed them when he began to work with an electric rock 'n' roll group. Folk fans had expected Dylan to continue making folk albums, but now he made a pop album, *Highway 61 Revisited*. But many pop fans, who had not enjoyed Dylan's music before, liked this new album. It was a very big hit and now even more people started to listen to Dylan.

Then Dylan had a bad motorbike accident in 1966. In this accident he broke his neck and was unable to sing and make records for more than two years. But he carried on writing songs, many of which were hits for other singers.

And he wrote a book as well, called *Tarantula*. It is a very difficult book to understand, but it showed that ideas and words were important to Dylan.

When he had recovered from his accident, he went back to work. Dylan's next two albums showed that his musical style had changed again. These albums, *John Wesley Harding* and *Nashville Skyline*, showed that he was now writing and singing in the style of country music.

In 1969, he made a successful appearance at the Isle of Wight festival. In 1971, he joined George Harrison and other pop stars at a free concert in New York. A really good album was made at this concert and we can hear Dylan singing some of his old songs, to the great delight of his fans in the audience.

His American tour with The Band in 1974 was so popular that it was almost impossible to get tickets for his concerts. More than ten years after his first record, Dylan is still one of the most important stars in pop music. What are the reasons for his great influence?

I think the answer is that he spoke for his generation through his songs and way of life. He understood and expressed the feelings of young people better than anyone else.

Before Dylan, it was believed that musicians should not make any comment on politics. Dylan changed this. He sang about Vietnam and racial prejudice[4]. Previously, young people had found no way to show what they themselves were thinking. Now, through Dylan's songs, they could express their own feelings.

His love songs were different, too. Most romantic songs are written without real feeling, often by middle-aged song-writers. Then a popular singer records the songs and tries very hard to make us believe that he is sincere.

But with Bob Dylan, you really felt that there was *A Girl from the North Country* (and there really was). You believed that *She Belongs to Me* was a song for a girl he really knew and loved. He had the courage to speak honestly about what he really believed. Most of all, he understood the feelings which he sang about and which were our feelings too.

SEVEN

FOLK

Bob Dylan created the folk movement and he was obviously the most important singer in folk music. Later his interest and influence moved away from folk and into pop music in general.

What really are the differences between folk and pop music? Folk-singers say that their songs are traditional[3] and come from the 'folk' or common people. The writers of these songs are often unknown and the songs have been sung for centuries.

Nobody knows who wrote most of the old blues songs, yet these songs are the real folk music of the black people in America. As well as the blues, folk music comes from the people of every race and country. Modern folk-singers also write folk songs in the style of the old, traditional songs.

Most folk-singers play an ordinary, non-electric guitar which they can carry around with them. In this way, they can make music whenever and wherever they want. Folk songs are usually well known and the audience can also join in and sing. Folk-singers prefer to sing in small clubs where the audience is small and friendly.

Bob Dylan also began his career in this way. In a part of New York called Greenwich Village, there are many small clubs and cafes. In these places, Dylan sang his songs to audiences of students, artists, writers and, sometimes, other folk-singers. Among those who listened to Dylan with great interest was a young student and singer called Joan Baez.

Joan Baez had a fine, clear voice and could play the guitar well. She also shared Bob Dylan's interest in the world around her. She, too, could see the changes in society, hated the war in Vietnam and the exploitation of black people in America.

Bob Dylan and Joan Baez liked and admired each other and at the beginning of their careers they often worked together. Dylan gave her many of his best songs to sing and she first became well-known through her records of Dylan's songs, like *Don't Think Twice – It's Alright* and *It Ain't Me, Babe.*

Many young people who enjoyed her songs also admired her for her intelligence and courage. Because of her beliefs, Joan Baez also took part in demonstrations against the Vietnam war. She was put in prison for joining a forbidden peace march. In the seventies, she is now spending more time on her political work and so has little time for singing or making records.

The influence of the Folk movement was much less in England. Young people in England had no war or race problem to protest about. But Dylan's way of singing, and even of dressing, had a strong effect on at least one young folk-singer is England. His name was Donovan Leitch.

At first, Donovan wore blue jeans and a cap like Dylan, and played the guitar and mouth organ like Dylan. He even sang like Dylan. Gradually, he began to find his own style and moved away from the influence of Bob Dylan. Some of the songs Donovan wrote in the mid-sixties are still popular. *Mellow Yellow* and *Sunshine Superman* are good songs because they are cheerful and full of melody.

Back in America, the Byrds were at first very much influenced by Bob Dylan, like Donovan and Joan Baez. But later the Byrds developed their own musical style. Their first song on record was *Mr Tambourine Man*, which was written by Dylan and was a great hit for them all over the world. They followed this success with another Dylan song, *All I Really Want To Do.*

In their songs, the Byrds tried to find a style which combined some of the qualities of Dylan and the Beatles.

And so they recorded folk songs, by Dylan himself or other folk-singers. At the same time, the group itself played electric guitars and sang in harmony[2] like the Beatles.

Later, the Byrds wrote and recorded their own songs, but the group did not seem to work together happily. Lots of musicians joined and then left the group, including David Crosby, who afterwards became famous with Crosby, Stills, Nash and Young. Although the Byrds made some good records in the late sixties and early seventies, they have never been able to equal the success of their first hit, *Mr Tambourine Man*.

Of all the singers and groups who were part of the Folk movement, only Simon and Garfunkel seemed to be unchanged by the influence of Bob Dylan. Simon and Garfunkel had their own style, which became stronger the more they worked together. Paul Simon wrote their songs and played the guitar with great skill.

Usually, they sang together in harmony, but sometimes Art Garfunkel would sing just by himself. When he sang alone, you could hear that he had a marvellous voice.

Although Paul Simon's music was very different from Bob Dylan's, there were some similarities in their early careers. Like Dylan, Paul Simon had studied English Literature at University and he tried to use words well in his songs. Paul Simon had also begun singing in the small clubs and cafes of New York, a couple of years after Dylan.

In his songs, Paul Simon writes about himself and his friends and his feelings about them. He and Bob Dylan often wrote songs about similar things, but Paul Simon's songs were never as angry as Dylan's. The voices of Simon and Garfunkel together perfectly expressed the gentleness and sadness of Paul Simon's songs.

Their first hit song was *The Sound of Silence*. Shortly after this success, Paul Simon was asked to write the music

41

Paul Simon.

'When you're weary, feeling small,
When tears are in your eyes, I will dry them all;
I'm on your side. When times get rough
And friends just can't be found,
Like a bridge over troubled water
I will lay me down.'

(from *Bridge Over Troubled Water*)

for the film *The Graduate*. That music, and especially the song *Mrs Robinson*, made Simon and Garfunkel really well known. In 1970 they had their greatest success with the album *Bridge Over Troubled Water*. During that summer it seemed impossible to turn on the radio without hearing the title song [2] and, four years later, the album was still in the charts.

By this time, Art Garfunkel had appeared in two films. He wanted to be an actor rather than a singer, so Simon and Garfunkel broke up. Paul Simon decided to continue as a solo singer [2] and he brought out his first album in 1972.

At the beginning of the sixties, a young Canadian poet was living and working on a small Greek island in the Mediterranean. His name was Leonard Cohen. In 1967, he put some of his poems to music and released an L.P. called *The Songs of Leonard Cohen*.

More and more people gradually heard and liked his songs, for example *Susanne* and *Bird on the Wire*. Now many of his songs have been recorded by other singers. Nowadays, the tickets for a Leonard Cohen concert are all sold almost as soon as they are put on sale.

Most folk-singers have been influenced to some extent by the blues, but Cohen's songs are different. He has never used blues rhythms or melodies and he prefers to tell a story in his songs. Since he is also a poet as well as a singer, his ideas and words are more complex than those of any other singer.

Leonard Cohen was the first of several Canadian folk-singers who became known in the late sixties. Another is Joni Mitchell and she writes and sings intelligent, personal and sometimes very funny songs. Her best known song is called *Clouds* – recorded and made famous by Judy Collins as *Both Sides Now*. Like all the best folk-singers, she uses well-written words with fine melodies.

In the early seventies, a song called *American Pie* suddenly appeared in the hit parade. It was written by a folk-singer called Don McLean, and the song tells the story of growing up in America during the fifties and sixties. The singer tells us how he used to listen to rock 'n' roll when he was a schoolboy and how, later, the Beatles, Bob Dylan and the Rolling Stones changed pop music.

'A long, long time ago –
I can still remember how that music used to make me smile
And I knew if I had my chance that I could make those people dance and maybe they'd be happy for a while.'

(from *American Pie*)

Don McLean's next big hit was *Vincent*, a fine song about the Dutch painter, Vincent Van Gogh. Both *Vincent* and *American Pie* were good pop songs because they had very attractive melodies, but *Vincent*, especially, was complex and unusual.

In the days of rock 'n' roll, before Bob Dylan and the folk movement, a song like *Vincent* would not have been a hit. Folk music, which was once played only in small cafes and clubs, had moved into the hit parade. Some people believe that the music we now call 'folk' is no longer folk music in its original sense. They may be right, but also there is no doubt that folk has greatly helped to make pop itself more interesting.

EIGHT

BLACK MUSIC

The blues have always been the most important part of black music and black people have sung the blues for many years. The blues had been a means of expressing many kinds of feelings. The singer, who usually played the guitar himself, sang about his troubles and his life in general.

In the fifties and sixties, the use of the electric guitar and other instruments made the blues into rhythm and blues. This new music was loud and rhythmic and made people want to dance when they heard it.

But the black people of the southern states of America also had another way to express their feelings. In the eighteenth and nineteenth centuries, they had accepted the Christian religion of their white masters.

The negroes sang the religious songs of Christianity and soon began to write their own songs, too. These religious songs were called 'spirituals'. The black people had their own style of singing, which was known as 'gospel'. The preacher or minister would sing a few words of the song and the people would sing together and repeat the same words. In this way they created a style of singing which they later used in non-religious music.

In the fifties, black singers brought the rhythms and feelings of the blues and added the enthusiasm and style of gospel music. Together, blues and gospel produced the kind of music known as 'soul'.

One of the first, and one of the greatest, of the soul singers was Ray Charles. Ray Charles was born in 1932. When he was only six, he became blind because his family was too poor to pay for medical treatment. In spite of his blindness, he learnt to play the piano. By the time he was a teenager, he was a full-time musician and made his first record at the age of seventeen.

Ray Charles had a voice which was perfect for singing the blues, and he played the piano marvellously. He influenced a great number of other singers, both black and white, and for many years he was the most popular black musician in the world. His greatest hit was a song he wrote himself called, *What I'd Say*. It sold millions of copies and was recorded by many other singers and groups.

Apart from Ray Charles and the rock 'n' roll singers, black music during the late fifties also included some popular groups, like the Drifters and the Coasters. Until the sixties, all the popular singers in America and England were solo singers. The black groups, with their skilful harmonies and sounds, showed that their kind of pop was also very enjoyable. They prepared the way for the British groups in the early sixties.

The best-known soul singers in the sixties were James Brown, Otis Redding and Aretha Franklin. Otis Redding was killed in a plane crash in 1967. At the time he was one of the most popular singers in the world and people continued to buy his records even after his death.

James Brown is the favourite singer of many black people, both in America and Africa. His concerts are famous because they are so exciting. His band plays the same basic rhythm, over and over again. James Brown himself has an extremely strong voice. He sings a few words, stops, and his band repeats the tune, using the traditional style of gospel music. Together, Brown and his band create tremendous excitement.

Aretha Franklin was probably the best woman soul singer. Her powerful singing was similar to the great blues singers like Bessie Smith and Mahalia Jackson. Aretha Franklin first began to sing in her father's church and her records had a deep sense of the blues and gospel music.

James Brown – the sound of soul music.

Her strong feeling for black music, together with her powerful voice, made her a great singer.

My own favourite singers are Ike and Tina Turner. They have been working together for more than ten years and during that time they have had one really great hit with a song called *River Deep, Mountain High*. Unfortunately, their records are not as exciting as their concerts. It is better to see them, if possible, rather than just listen to them on record.

Soul music was one way in which black people brought the qualities of their own music into pop music.

In the sixties also, another kind of black music, called 'Tamla Motown', became popular very quickly. Soon it was as well-known as 'soul' music. Although both kinds of music belonged to the black people of America, the musical style of soul and Tamla Motown were quite different.

The word 'motown' is a short form of the words 'motor town'. The home of this kind of music was Detroit, where the Ford motor company had its biggest factory. There were many black workers in the motor industry in Detroit. They had come from the southern states to find work in the factories of the north. They brought with them their great liking for music, especially the blues.

In Detroit, in the late fifties, an unknown black singer, whose name was Berry Gordy, wrote and recorded a song called *Money – That's What I Want*. Although not many people heard Gordy's original record, it reached the Beatles in Liverpool. *Money* was one of the first songs the Beatles ever recorded.

Gordy built a small recording studio with the money he received from his song. He wrote more songs and began to produce records of the best known black groups and singers in Detroit. Gordy had realised that a lot of white people enjoyed the dancing rhythms of black music. He knew, too, that he could make much more money

48

Diana Ross – Tamla Motown's most glamorous star.

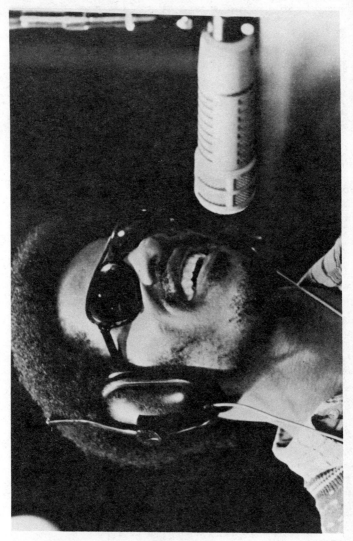

Stevie Wonder.

if his records were bought by both white and black people.

His company, now called Tamla Motown, started to produce a kind of dance music that most people could enjoy. Their music was very rhythmic and had clever harmonies. But, because most white people did not like or understand the blues, Tamla Motown did not use the blues as part of their music.

Diana Ross and the Supremes were the most successful Tamla Motown singers. After they had had a dozen hits together, Diana Ross left the Supremes and is now both a singing star and a film star. Many other groups and singers began their careers with Tamla Motown, including the Four Tops, the Temptations and Stevie Wonder.

In the seventies, Stevie Wonder has become a really creative singer and musician. Other black musicians have turned away from the influence of Tamla Motown because they believe it is not the true music of black people. Now, writers and singers like Isaac Hayes and Curtis Mayfield are trying to create music to express the real feelings of black people.

Towards the end of the sixties, another kind of black music began to influence pop. The black people of the West Indies had their own kind of popular music, called 'reggae'. In the fifties, like everybody else, West Indians heard a lot of rhythm and blues. They accepted it and local musicians began to add rhythm and blues to their own musical styles. They also started to use electric guitars and bass to play the new kind of music called reggae.

Reggae has only really become well known in the seventies, mainly through the records of Johnny Nash and Jimmy Cliff. Several American pop singers have used reggae musicians on their records. Paul Simon, the Rolling Stones and Cat Stevens have all recorded songs in Jamaica with local musicians.

Reggae is only one of the many kinds of black music. I have already discussed jazz, the blues, gospel and soul music and Tamla Motown. In my own opinion, the music of black people in general has been the strongest and most important influence on pop music as a whole.

NINE

THE MUSIC INDUSTRY

I have been using various words like 'rock 'n' roll', 'rhythm 'n' blues' and 'soul'. These are different kinds of music which together have helped to make pop. But what about the word 'pop' itself? What does that word really mean? The word 'pop' is a short form of popular, and so we must ask ourselves what popular music really is.

For many people, pop simply means the records which are in the hit parade at that moment and which they hear regularly on the radio. Pop singers are the singers they see on television and read about in their daily newspaper. But, if we look closely at the facts, we see that the situation is not quite so simple.

The most successful recording stars of all time are the Beatles. But, apart from them, the best-selling records have always been albums like *The Sound of Music*, or songs from the Eurovision Song Contest[2]. In addition, each country has its own popular singers whose records do not usually sell outside that country.

The pop music I have been talking about in this book is really the music of young people. But not only the young like records; their parents buy records, too. Older people are less influenced by changes in musical fashion and usually prefer songs which are familiar rather than new or unknown. They like music which is easy to listen to and which is not too loud or rhythmic. And so pop includes very different kinds of music from the most progressive[3] to the most familiar and well-known.

The words 'charts' and 'hit parade' have also been used, and both words mean the list of best-selling records of the moment. But there are really two kinds of charts. The hit parade itself is a list of the most popular singles. A single is a record with only two songs, the one which most people want to listen to on the 'A' side, and another, less important song on the 'B' side.

For many people, pop music means the hit parade. But another chart, the list of best-selling <u>albums</u>, often gives a different picture of what is happening in pop. Albums are much more expensive than singles and, during a week or month, an album will not sell in such great numbers as a single. But, over a longer period of time, an album may actually sell more copies than a single.

An album has important advantages for a serious musician. A single lasts three or four minutes, but an album lasts much longer. <u>A musician has more time on an album to express his musical ideas.</u> Also a single usually stays in the charts for about ten or twelve weeks, but an album <u>lasts</u> much longer. <u>For example, we can still buy the first records of Bob Dylan and the Beatles, more than ten years after they were made.</u>

A young person who is going to buy an album usually thinks very carefully about his choice. If he buys an album that he does not really like, then he has made quite an expensive mistake. If he buys a single and does not like it, he has not wasted so much money. And so, when he is buying an album, a young person will look for one that he can enjoy for a long time.

Many musicians have realised the advantages of making albums. Groups like Pink Floyd, Deep Purple and Emerson, Lake and Palmer release[2] only albums, sometimes double or even <u>triple albums</u>. Other groups, for example Procol Harum or Rod Stewart and the Faces, prefer to make albums, but occasionally release a good, popular single.

The business of making a record can be quite complicated. A group or singer usually needs about twelve songs for an album. They may write their own songs, or have the songs specially written for them; or they may

choose older songs which they like. When a group have
gathered enough songs for the album, they go into the
recording studio.

A group sometimes has to work in the recording studio
for many weeks to complete an album, although an album
can sometimes be recorded 'live'[2] at a concert. Perhaps the
group also needs some extra musicians or 'session men' as
they are called, to help in the recording.

Session men are among the most important people in
pop although their names are not well known. They are
musicians with a lot of experience and great skill. They
can often play more than one instrument. They help
the group to make the record, but their names do not often
appear on the record because they are not members of
the group.

For example, on the Beatles' first record, Ringo Starr
did not play the drums, which were in fact played by a
session man. Other pop stars, like Jimmy Page of Led
Zeppelin, began their musical careers as session men and
later became famous with a group.

In addition to session men, the group in the studio
needs a producer and an 'A and R man'. The A and R
man arranges dates and makes sure everybody is avail-
able. He also deals with all the little problems during
recording. The producer makes decisions about the music
itself.

The producer decides which instruments to use on the
record. The producer is also in charge of 'mixing'. Mixing
means putting all the different sounds together to make a
record. Very often a group records each instrument separately. Then the producer mixes the different instruments
to produce the final sound.

This technique of 'mixing' allows one man to make a
record on which he plays all the instruments. A very
famous example is Mike Oldfield's *Tubular Bells*. First of
all he recorded the guitar part. Then he added the sounds

of other instruments to this recording until he had completed the record.

Before a completed record can be offered for sale, a 'sleeve' has to be designed. The sleeve is the cover of the record. On it are the names of the songs and the musicians and perhaps other information about the record. Usually, a commercial artist designs the sleeve, but occasionally a singer or member of the group likes to do it. Bob Dylan, for example, drew the picture on his album *Self Portrait*. The drawings on Ringo Starr's album *Ringo* are by Klaus Voormann, who played on the record itself.

Then the record is ready for the public. Copies of the record are sent to disc-jockeys, who then play the record on the radio and perhaps comment on it. Sometimes the record company puts advertisements in the papers. But the success of the record depends finally on the public, who decide whether to buy it or not.

If enough people buy the record, it enters the charts and is played many times on the radio. Each time we hear a record on the radio, it earns money for three kinds of people: the record company, the song-writers and the group or singer. The record company gets the biggest share and the singer the least. Sometimes the singer is also the song-writer and in this way he can earn more money.

Money has always been one of the biggest influences in pop, whether we like it or not. For example, it was the rich American teenagers who first made rock 'n' roll popular. And in the seventies, too, money continues to influence the kind of music we can listen to.

TEN

MORE ABOUT THE BEATLES

During the early sixties, the Beatles had made one hit after another and in 1967 they released their famous album, *Sergeant Pepper's Lonely Hearts Club Band.* By now they were the richest and best known group in pop music. Other groups imitated them. For example, the Beatles started to use an Indian instrument called the sitar, and

Beatle George Harrison (right) with Ravi Shankar and other Indian musicians in 1970.

The Beatles with family, friends and the Maharishi.

very soon lots of other pop groups were using the sitar, too.

All the time, the whole world read and talked about everything they did. Newspapers reported all their actions and opinions. The public was told what they wore, what they ate, where they lived and, even, who they were in love with. They made two successful films, *A Hard Day's Night* and *Help*, and John Lennon had written two best-selling books, *In His Own Write* and *A Spaniard in the Works*. The Beatles had even received a decoration from the Queen of England in 1965.

And then, in June 1967, they released *Sergeant Pepper*. More people than ever before bought this album, but the record was really important for other reasons. *Sergeant Pepper* introduced new influences which changed pop music.

The Beatles had obviously been listening to Bob Dylan's songs, especially those about the problems of ordinary people. One of the songs in *Sergeant Pepper* is called *She's Leaving Home*; it tells us about a young girl who could not get on with her parents. She decides to run away and she leaves them sad and unable to understand why she has gone.

'Wednesday morning at five o'clock as
the day begins
Silently closing her bedroom door
Leaving the note that she hoped would
say more
She goes downstairs to the kitchen
clutching her handkerchief
Quietly turning the backdoor key
Stepping outside she is free.'

(from *She's Leaving Home*)

In the same album, George Harrison's song, *Within You, Without You*, shows his interest in Indian music. Just before they made the record, the Beatles had been studying Indian music and religion. George Harrison had visited India in 1966 and had played the sitar with the great Indian musician, Ravi Shankar. Just after releasing *Sergeant Pepper*, the Beatles spent some time with the Maharishi Mahesh Yogi, an Indian religious teacher.

Before they became interested in Indian religion, the Beatles had used drugs. 1967 was the 'Hippie' summer, when 'Flower Power' was a new and hopeful idea. Suddenly, we all heard about the Hippie ideas of love and peace. It was also well known that many Hippies smoked a drug called 'Hash', which was their name for cannabis or marijuana.

John Lennon once explained how the Beatles started to take drugs. He said that when the Beatles were working in Germany, they often had to play for eight hours or more. They usually worked until four or five o'clock in the morning. In order to keep awake, they took certain kinds of drugs.

After their first hit record in England, the Beatles made many tours and gave many concerts. On tour, they worked late into the night and then had to get up early to travel to the next concert. All the time they were staying in hotels, eating and sleeping in a hurry. The Beatles – and many other pop groups like them – took drugs to help them sleep or wake up, or just to make them feel less tired.

In England and America during the early sixties, young people began to use the drug, cannabis. People smoked cannabis because they thought that it helped them to relax. But smoking cannabis was against the law, and various pop musicians were arrested by the police for using this drug.

L.S.D., called 'acid' by most people, is a much stronger

and more dangerous drug than cannabis. It is said to change a person's mind so much that he sees everything differently. John Lennon explained that he first took acid by chance: somebody put it on the sugar which he then put in his coffee. He drank his cup of coffee without knowing that it contained acid. Many people think that the song in *Sergeant Pepper*, *Lucy in the Sky with Diamonds*, is about L.S.D.

In America, the use of acid started a type of music known as 'Acid Rock'. In California, where the Hippie movement had begun, a lot of musicians took acid regularly, because they believed that it helped them to make better music. Several singers had written songs about the effects of acid. The best known of these songs is *Mr Tambourine Man* by Bob Dylan.

In making their album, *Sergeant Pepper*, the Beatles used their knowledge of Indian music and the new freedom which allowed them to write about all kinds of events and ideas. Although the record contained lots of new and unusual music, it succeeded because the Beatles always wrote memorable and tuneful songs.

During 1967, the Beatles also made some marvellous single records, like *Penny Lane*, *Strawberry Fields Forever* and *All You Need Is Love*. However, that Christmas they had their first failure with a film called *Magical Mystery Tour*. The film was shown on television in 1967, but most people found it too difficult to understand.

Although *Magical Mystery Tour* contained four new Lennon and McCartney songs, the film was disappointing. The film was the Beatles' first production after the death, in September 1967, of their manager, Brian Epstein. Despite the failure of *Magical Mystery Tour*, they decided not to look for another manager. Instead, they formed their own company, which they called 'Apple'.

The Beatles wanted to make their own records and their first record with Apple was *Hey Jude*. They also wanted to find and help new singers and song-writers. For example, Paul McCartney produced Mary Hopkin's great hit *Those were the Days*. Apple succeeded in making good records, but in other ways the company lost money and became a problem for the Beatles.

In the meantime, a lot of other things had happened. In 1968, John Lennon met a Japanese artist called Yoko Ono, whom he later married. They made films and records together, without the other Beatles. But their work was difficult and unusual and people did not understand it. In the same year, John Lennon and Yoko Ono were arrested and fined for having drugs.

Ringo Starr also made a record by himself but not many people bought it. George Harrison was studying Indian music and wrote music for films. Paul McCartney had also written film music. While working in America, he had met an American girl, Linda Eastmann. They got married in March 1969. On the same day, George Harrison and his wife were arrested for having drugs.

The Beatles seemed to be in trouble. They had their own personal problems and they also had financial worries with Apple. Each Beatle was now trying to do different things with his music. The *White* album, which was released late in 1968, shows how the musical ideas of each member of the group were growing apart.

The Beatles' last record together was *Abbey Road*. The most popular songs on that album were *Something* and *Here Comes the Sun*, and both were written by George Harrison. The whole album was very enjoyable, but we did not know then that the Beatles would only be together for a few more months.

One day, in July 1970, it was announced that the Beatles had finally broken up. That evening, the radio played all their great records. I sat up, listening to that marvellous music. Like everybody else, I was sorry that the Beatles had broken up, but I felt more grateful than sad. If you, too, know the music they made between 1962 and 1970, you will understand why I felt grateful that night.

ELEVEN

WOODSTOCK

Woodstock was the biggest and most famous pop festival of the sixties. It took place in 1969 in the small town of Woodstock in the state of New York. The town stands in the middle of fields and farms. Bob Dylan had seen the beauty of this countryside and had come to Woodstock to recover after his motorbike accident. It seemed a fine place to hold a pop festival.

The planning of the festival took a long time. At first, it was difficult to get the permission of the local people to hold a festival on their land. Many of the farmers were afraid that the enormous crowds would damage their fields and property. Later, when the festival took place, these people were surprised by the good behaviour of the pop fans.

The organisers of the festival wanted to invite the best pop groups and singers in the world. After many letters and phone calls, some of the most famous names in pop had agreed to play at Woodstock, and the organisers were able to prepare for the festival.

First, they had to find a good position for the festival. They needed a water supply, electricity and enough space for an enormous number of pop fans to sleep, eat and listen to the music. Then they had to have a large stage, with a powerful sound system.

It was quite a big problem to arrange the sound system. Each group or singer used different kinds of instruments. Some singers, like Joan Baez, needed only a microphone, but other groups, for example Sly and the Family Stone, had nine musicians. Groups like these needed a great deal of equipment and lots of microphones and speakers.

A few weeks before the festival, an army of builders

moved into Woodstock. They worked hard to supply water and electricity. They built the stage, washrooms and showers, and a shopping area where the pop fans could buy food and drinks. They also built a large fence round the whole festival site.

For days before the opening of the festival, pop fans came to Woodstock from all over America. Some even came from outside America! They travelled by car, by bus and by train, but many more hitch-hiked and a few even walked. More than half a million people were at Woodstock, and millions more saw the film which was made at the festival.

The young people who came to Woodstock found that they shared other interests, as well as their love for music. They belonged to a generation of young people who believed that they could all enjoy themselves peacefully together. They believed in peace and friendship. The newspapers had said that violent and greedy pop fans might spoil Woodstock, but these young people proved the newspapers wrong. The festival was a great success.

A few months after Woodstock, I spoke to a young American pop fan who had been there. First of all, I asked him why he had gone to Woodstock. He thought about my question for a few moments and then he began to reply.

'I think I went,' he said, 'because it was so different from my usual life.'

'Why?' I asked. 'What's your job?'

'I work in an office with computers,' he replied. 'I've been doing the same job since I left college, about eighteen months ago. Woodstock was so free and relaxed after working in an office.'

'Did you only go there for the freedom?' I asked him.

'No, it was more than just that,' he explained. 'I really like pop music. I first began to listen to pop music when I heard rock 'n' roll on the radio. Then I bought a record player and began to buy records. So, of course, I already had lots of records by the Who, and Crosby, Stills, Nash and Young and Joan Baez. And now I had this great chance to see them at Woodstock.'

Then I asked him if he had really enjoyed the festival.

'Yes, very much,' he replied. 'I met a lot of pleasant people there. We liked the same kind of music and most of us had the same ideas about society.'

'What kind of ideas do you mean?' I asked.

'We just wanted to be free, ourselves,' he said, 'and to let other people live the way they wanted. It seems, nowadays, that too many people like to control other peoples' lives for them.'

We talked for a long time about Woodstock – about the music, and also about the beliefs of the young people who had gone there. Although the festival had been a great experience for my friend, there had been some problems as well. I asked him what the biggest problem had been.

'The rain,' he answered. 'One day it rained all afternoon and evening. It was damp and miserable and we couldn't really sleep.'

'Didn't that make people bad-tempered and angry?' I asked.

'Oh, no!' he exclaimed. 'Just the opposite. Because of the rain, we all tried to keep each other cheerful. We built fires, cooked food, drank coffee. The musicians played longer, too, so that we wouldn't feel so miserable.'

Like most people, I only saw Woodstock in the cinema, but even on film it seemed a great event. Fortunately, the best moments of the festival were also recorded, and so we can listen again to Joe Cocker's *With a Little Help from my Friends* or the Who's *My Generation*. Most of all, I remember the playing of Ten Years After and Jimi Hendrix.

Woodstock and the concert in the Isle of Wight were the last great festivals in pop. The late sixties had been a

40,000 fans at a pop festival in Lancashire, England in 1972. Permission to hold a festival can be hard to get.

time of hope and the young people who had gone to Woodstock had expressed their hopes for peace and a freer world. Many of the young people at the festival had also joined demonstrations to ask their government to stop the war in Vietnam. Despite their protests, America was still at war.

In the late sixties, also, student movements grew up throughout the world. But everywhere – in Paris, in Mexico City, in Prague – the police had tried to stop these demonstrations. The politicians in these countries refused to listen to students and carried on as usual. The songs of hope and protest were forgotten.

Pop festivals showed very clearly that young people wanted to choose their own way of life. As well as a festival of music, Woodstock was an example of another way of life. The newspapers quickly compared pop festivals with the student movements in various countries. In the same way as they had stopped the student demonstrations, the authorities tried to stop the festivals.

The politicians and the police said that festivals were dirty and dangerous, and that the crowds of fans left the countryside full of bottles, paper and empty tins. The police said that traffic could not move easily and that public transport could not carry such great numbers of people. It was said that the local people complained about the noise. For of all these reasons, it became almost impossible to get permission to hold a festival.

During the pop festival at Altamont, a Hell's Angel had killed a young pop fan and this gave the authorities an even stronger reason to stop other festivals. It was well known, too, that many young people took drugs with them to the festivals. The police were determined to stop young people buying and selling drugs. And so the festivals disappeared.

Occasionally, somebody has managed to get permission to hold a pop festival. Local people read in their newspapers that there are going to be enormous numbers of wild young pop fans, buying and selling drugs and fighting. Naturally, the local people do not welcome the festival, and there are always lots of policemen there, ready for trouble.

When everybody works together and helps each other, pop festivals are happy events. When everybody expects trouble, nobody can enjoy either the festival or the music. Unfortunately, it looks as if there will be no more happy festivals. Woodstock was probably the last of the great pop festivals.

TWELVE

INTO THE SEVENTIES

Towards the end of the sixties, important changes began to take place in pop music. Many of the best groups had already broken up or were just about to break up. These included the Beatles, Cream, the Mamas and Papas, Crosby, Stills, Nash and Young and Creedence Clearwater Revival. Worse was to come.

In the early seventies, Duane Allmann, of the Allmann Brothers, was killed in a motorbike accident. And Janis Joplin, Jimi Hendrix and Jim Morrison of the Doors all died. Nobody really knows why these three singers died, although it was known that each of them sometimes took drugs. When people read about these deaths in the newspapers, they wonder why a famous and skilful musician risks his or her life with drugs.

Pop stars earn a great deal of money, but they also spend a lot. They have to buy expensive equipment and pay their musicians. Also, travelling and touring costs them a lot of money. To pay for all these different expenses they have to sell a large number of records.

But money is not the only problem. Some stars, like Jimi Hendrix, never really enjoyed the music which they had to play in public and on record. Nor did they like the public 'image' which they had too keep up. An 'image' is the idea that the public has of a star, through newspapers, films and television. Often, this image is very different from the real person. Some stars enjoy keeping up an image for their fans. Others, like Jimi Hendrix, found the problem was too much for them.

With the death of Hendrix and other stars, pop music lost a lot of talented musicians. In addition many other musicians were no longer working in pop music for various reasons. For a short time, pop was in trouble. But soon, new singers and groups appeared, and some of the old stars returned to show that they were still good.

For example, the four Beatles are again making music, each in his own different way. George Harrison had a great hit in 1970 with *My Sweet Lord* and his triple album, released in the same year, was also a great success. Paul McCartney has written a lot of songs and formed his own group, called Wings.

John Lennon's ability to continue writing and singing good songs, like *Imagine*, is well-known. One of his songs, *How Do You Sleep*, is about the quarrels between John and Paul which partly caused the break up of the Beatles. Ringo still enjoys making happy music, and his album, *Ringo*, was one of the best-selling records of 1974.

The Who have also continued to make good music. Their concerts are among the most exciting in pop and, for many people, their *Quadrophenia* was the best-written and best-made album of 1974. Another great group of the sixties, the Rolling Stones, have stayed together into the seventies, making records and giving concerts.

Bob Dylan, too, has gone back to work and in 1974 he made his first tour for more than seven years. He went on tour with the Band, the group which played with him on his great records of the sixties. The Band, whether working with Dylan or just by themselves, make some of the best music in pop.

The Beach Boys are still playing and giving pleasure to many people, while some of the great rock 'n' roll stars of the fifties are enjoying new popularity. Chuck Berry, for example, is working harder than ever and has appeared in films with Little Richard, Jerry Lee Lewis and Bo Diddley.

If we compare the hit parades of the sixties with those of the seventies, we can see clearly that solo singers have come back into pop music. During the sixties, a few solo singers, such as Tom Jones, were popular, but most successful records were by groups.

Now, in the seventies, lots of solo singers also write their own songs. Most of these singers, like Melanie and Carly Simon, are new names in pop music. But one of the best singer/song-writers is Carole King, who first began to write songs in the early sixties with her husband, Gerry Goffin. Together, they wrote lots of hits for other singers and groups.

Suddenly, in 1970, Carole King released an album on which she sang her own songs. The album was called *Tapestry*, and was bought by more than four million people. She still writes good songs for other people, too, like *You've Got a Friend*, which was a big hit for James Taylor.

A song-writer understands his own songs better than anybody else and so he usually sings them with more real feeling than other singers. If an unknown song-writer writes a good song, he may give it to a well-known group to record. In that way, the song has a good chance of being a hit. The song-writer will earn more money than if he had tried to record the song himself.

Cat Stevens and Neil Diamond, for example, both wrote hit songs for other people in the sixties. Neil Diamond had written songs for the Monkees for three or four years before he had his first big success in 1970 with his own song, *Sweet Caroline*. In the seventies, Cat Stevens has become one of the most successful singers in pop music.

The most popular, and perhaps the most talented of the new singer/song-writers is Elton John. He has had one hit album after another, each album full of good songs. Elton John writes the music and Bernie Taupin writes the words. Whenever he gives a concert, Elton John appears on stage wearing extraordinary clothes and strange

Elton John, exciting to watch and to listen to.

Elton John, showing his taste for unusual and colourful clothes.

glasses. He believes that pop music should be exciting to watch as well as to listen to.

Elton John's taste for wearing unusual and colourful clothes follows a fashion which was started in 1970 by Marc Bolan. The pop stars of the sixties had usually preferred to wear blue jeans to any other kind of clothes. Marc Bolan decided that it was time for a change. He began to wear colourful, unusual clothes and wore heavy make-up on his face. Because his appearance was so unusual, he soon became well-known and other singers very quickly followed his example. Gary Glitter, the Slade and the Sweet are some of the pop stars of the seventies whose appearance and actions on stage have helped to bring them success.

When Alice Cooper and David Bowie give concerts, they both try to excite their audience in different ways. Cooper takes a snake with him on stage and wears black make-up and extremely strange clothes. David Bowie has studied the art of mime [4] and so his live concerts are very dramatic and unusual.

During the seventies also, a kind of pop known as 'heavy' music has gained a lot of fans among the young. In the late sixties, Cream was the first of the heavy groups. Heavy music is based on the blues, but gives the musicians a lot of opportunity to improvise [2]. Improvisation needs great skill and imagination; only a few groups, like the Cream had that skill.

When Cream broke up, many other groups tried to create the same kind of music. In America, groups like Blood, Sweat and Tears and Chicago have made some good records, while in England the most popular heavy groups are Black Sabbath, Deep Purple and Led Zeppelin.

The story of pop music in the seventies also includes the new stars like the Osmonds and David Cassidy. Pop music is now a part of many peoples' lives. This is especially true of the growing number of young fans who

Alice Cooper. . . .

A long way from the stars of the fifties and sixties.

have discovered their own, younger stars in Donny Osmond and David Cassidy.

The Osmonds began singing as a group when they were very small boys in the mid-sixties. They are advised by their parents, who also taught them music. The Osmonds are clean and polite and play pleasant music. Parents like them and are happy to give their children money to buy the Osmonds' records. In this way, the Osmonds are very different from a group like the Rolling Stones and their fans are different too.

*

We have seen many changes in pop since the fifties affecting the stars, the music, the fans. But one thing has not changed; pop stars today face the same problem they faced in the fifties and sixties. The problem is to be both popular and musically exciting. It can be done. The Beatles and Bob Dylan, for example, did it. They made marvellous music which millions of people enjoyed. For me, that is really the story of pop.

POINTS FOR UNDERSTANDING

CHAPTER 1

1. In 1957, the first rock 'n' roll American singer came to England. Who was he?
2. What song marked the beginning of pop?
3. Why did teenagers in the fifties have to listen to the same music as their parents?
4. What was important about the film, *The Blackboard Jungle*?

CHAPTER 2

1. What were the reactions of parents to the rock 'n' roll movement?
2. What was the name for the style of dancing to rock 'n' roll?
3. What do you understand by the phrase, 'the Generation Gap'?
4. Who were 'Teddy Boys' and why were they given this name?

CHAPTER 3

1. Where did blues music come from?
2. Why were white people at first shocked by jazz?
3. With the invention of the electric guitar, a new kind of music based on the blues was developed. What was it called?
4. What part did radio stations play in the spread of black music?
5. Rock 'n' roll is a mixture of two kinds of music. What are they?

CHAPTER 4

1. What was the Beatles' first record?
2. What was 'The Cavern'?
3. Which two people helped the Beatles most in their early careers?
4. Which Beatles' song sold most records?

CHAPTER 5

1. Why were young people in Liverpool able to get hold of American records?
2. What was the strongest musical influence in the Rolling Stones' first records?
3. What was the Rolling Stones' first hit and who had originally sung it?
4. Why did some journalists describe the Rolling Stones as 'rebels against society'?
5. Which member of the Rolling Stones died in 1969?
6. What went wrong at Altamont?
7. What are the Who's two most famous works?

CHAPTER 6

1. Why did Robert Zimmerman choose the name 'Dylan'?
2. What was unusual about Dylan's voice and his way of playing the mouth organ?
3. What is Dylan saying in his song, *The Times They Are A-Changin'*?
4. 'Dylan made words important.' Explain.
5. Why did many fans of folk music think that Dylan betrayed them when he began to work with The Band?

CHAPTER 7

1. What kind of feelings did Joan Baez try to express in the words of her songs?
2. Why was the influence of the folk movement less strong in England then in America?
3. What was the Byrds' first hit and who wrote it?
4. Who made the following folk songs famous – *Mellow Yellow*, *Bridge Over Troubled Water*, *American Pie*, *Suzanne*?

CHAPTER 8

Soul, Tamla Motown and reggae are three popular types of black music. Which types of black music are the following singers famous for:

    (a) Johnny Nash
    (b) Diana Ross and the Supremes
    (c) Otis Redding
    (d) Jimmy Cliff
    (e) Aretha Franklin

CHAPTER 9

Explain the meaning of the following words used in the music industry:

    (a) hit parade
    (b) session man
    (c) triple album
    (d) 'A' side of a single
    (e) mixing
    (f) sleeve
    (g) disc-jockey

CHAPTER 10

1. What famous album did the Beatles release in 1967?
2. Who was the Maharishi Mahesh Yogi?
3. What reasons did the Beatles give for first taking drugs?
4. What happened to the Beatles in July 1970?

CHAPTER 11

1. What was the most important and successful pop festival of the sixties?
2. What kind of ideas about society were shared by the fans who came to this festival?
3. Why did the authorities object to pop festivals?

CHAPTER 12

1. After they broke up, the Beatles continued to make music separately. What has each one done since 1969?
2. Which group from the sixties produced the album *Quadrophenia* in 1974?
3. Which star began the fashion for wearing unusual and colourful clothes in 1970?
4. What are unusual about the concerts of Alice Cooper and David Bowie?
5. 'Pop stars today face the same problem they faced in the fifties and sixties.' What is the problem?

GLOSSARY

Pop consists of many types of music and these are discussed and explained throughout the book. The following is a list of these types of music:

acid rock	reggae
blues	rhythm 'n' blues ('n' = and)
folk	rock 'n' roll
gospel	soul
heavy music .	spiritual
jazz	Tamla Motown

SECTION 2

Terms to do with music and the music industry

album (page 32)

a number of songs recorded together on the same long playing record. A double or triple album is where there are two or three records together.

business – music business (page 11)

see under *industry – music industry*.

charts (page 18)

the list of best selling records. See Chapter Nine for further discussion.

contest – Eurovision Song Contest (page 53)

a yearly televised competition between countries in Western Europe to find the best pop song.

copy (page 6)

a record.

fans (page 1)

> people who take a great interest in a singer or pop group.

folk (page 12)

> songs of ordinary people. The writers of the words and music are often unknown. With Bob Dylan, the 'Folk Movement' began – a particular type of music within pop.

harmony (page 41)

> playing or singing music so that the different instruments or voices join together in a pleasant way.

hit (page 15)

> a best selling record. See also 'hit parade'.

improvise (page 75)

> to change and develop a piece of music while you are playing it.

industry – music industry (page 21)

> the music industry or business refers to all the money-making activities of making music. See Chapter Nine for further discussion.

influence (page 15)

> rock 'n' roll was influenced by country music. The sounds of country music helped to shape and make the music which we call rock 'n' roll. To influence something is to help to create it or to change it.

live – to record live (page 55)

> to record on stage in front of an audience and not in

L.P. (page 20)

> Long Playing record. See 'album'.

melodies (page 12)

> simple tunes.

parade – hit parade (page 15)

> a list of the best selling records. See also 'charts'.

pop (page 2)

    a short form of the word 'popular'.

release – release a record (page 54)

    to put a record out for sale in record shops.

rhythms – regular rhythms (page 12)

    music which has certain strong beats which come regularly. The kind of music which makes you want to beat time with your hands or feet.

singer – solo singer (page 43)

    one person singing by himself or herself.

song – title song (page 43)

    the name of the song which is used for the name of the album. For example, the title song of the album *Bridge Over Troubled Water* is the song of the same name.

talent – musical talent (page 25)

    a great ability to write or to play music.

tour (page 6)

    when a singer or group play in concerts in different cities.

works (page 30)

    pieces of music – usually longer pieces of music which are considered important.

SECTION 3

Adjectives used to describe music and musicians

complex – complex feelings (page 36)

    feelings that are difficult to explain.

familiar – familiar music (page 15)

    well-known music.

fashioned – old-fashioned (page 4)

    old songs which have no interest and excitement for younger people.

original – original form of jazz (page 12)
> the first way in which jazz music was played.

outstanding – outstanding groups (page 25)
> very able and successful groups.

rhythmic – rhythmic jazz (page 12)
> jazz with a strong, regular beat.

progressive – progressive music (page 53)
> new, developing type of music, usually difficult to understand. It is not simply meant to sound pleasing.

romantic – romantic music (page 3)
> sweet, simple music. Most romantic songs are about love.

traditional – traditional jazz (page 39)
> well-known songs from a past age.

SECTION 4

Other words

Carnaby Street (page 30)
> famous London street, particularly in 1960s, full of boutiques selling modern clothes.

exploitation (page 35)
> unfair treatment of people by governments or men in power.

prejudice – racial prejudice (page 37)
> strong and unreasonable feelings of dislike for other people because they are of a different race.

mime – the art of mime (page 75)
> acting on the stage without speaking.

Acknowledgements

The author and publishers are grateful to the following for permission to reproduce photographs and words from songs:

MGM Records, *The Osmonds*, page 2.

Keystone Press Agency Ltd, pages 3, 7, 9, 19, 29, 57, 58 and 67.

RCA Ltd, *Elvis Presley*, page 16.

Phonogram Ltd, *Chuck Berry*, page 17.

Mike Putnam and Atlantic Records, *The Rolling Stones*, page 26.

CBS Records Ltd, *Bob Dylan*, page 33, and *Paul Simon*, page 42.

Polydor Ltd, *James Brown*, page 47.

EMI Records Ltd, (Motown Records Co.,) *Diana Ross*, page 49 and *Stevie Wonder*, page 50.

Caroline Boucher and Rocket Record Co. Ltd, *Elton John*, pages 73 and 74.

Warner Bros. Music Ltd, *Alice Cooper*, pages 76 and 77.

ATV Music Ltd, for permission to reproduce lines from 'I Want to Hold Your Hand', John Lennon & Paul McCartney, (1963), page 22 and lines from 'She's Leaving Home', John Lennon and Paul McCartney (1967) from the L.P. *Sergeant Pepper's Lonely Hearts Club Band*, page 59.

Warner Bros. Music Ltd, for permission to reproduce lines from 'The Times They Are A-Changin'', Bob Dylan, page 34.

Pattern Music Ltd, for permission as publishers, to reproduce lines from 'Bridge Over Troubled Water',